Disney · PIXAR

Learn to Draw

TOY STORY

WOODY & FRIENDS

Walter Foster Jr.

This library edition published in 2020 by Walter Foster Jr.,
an imprint of The Quarto Group
26391 Crown Valley Parkway, Suite 220
Mission Viejo, CA 92691, USA.

Step art by the Disney Storybook Artists and Pablo Mendoza.

Distributed in the United States and Canada by
Lerner Publisher Services
241 First Avenue North
Minneapolis, MN 55401 U.S.A.
www.lernerbooks.com

First Library Edition

Library of Congress Cataloging-in-Publication Data

Title: Learn to draw Disney/Pixar Toy story. Woody & friends.
Description: First library edition. | Mission Viejo, CA : Walter Foster Jr.,
    an imprint of The Quarto Group, 2020. | Audience: Ages: 6+. | Audience:
    Grades: 4-6.
Identifiers: LCCN 2019017172 | ISBN 9781600588341 (hardcover)
Subjects: LCSH: Cartoon characters--Juvenile literature. | Toy story
    films--Juvenile literature. | Drawing--Technique--Juvenile literature.
Classification: LCC NC1764 .L3345 2020 | DDC 741.5/1--dc23 LC record available
    at https://lccn.loc.gov/2019017172

Printed in USA
9 8 7 6 5 4 3 2 1

Table of Contents

How to Use This Book 4

Drawing Exercises 5

Woody 6

Buzz Lightyear 8

The Prospector 10

Lotso 16

Big Baby... 22

Chunk 26

Mr. Pricklepants 30

Buttercup 34

Bo Peep 38

Forky 44

Duke Caboom 48

Ducky & Bunny 54

Gabby Gabby 58

How to Use This Book

Just follow these simple steps, and you'll be amazed at how fun and easy drawing can be!

1 Draw the basic shape of the character; then add simple guidelines to help you place the features.

2 Each new step is shown in blue. Simply follow the blue lines to add the details.

3 Erase any lines you don't want to keep.

4 Use crayons, markers, colored pencils, or paints to add color.

Drawing Exercises

Warm up your hand by drawing lots of squiggles and shapes.

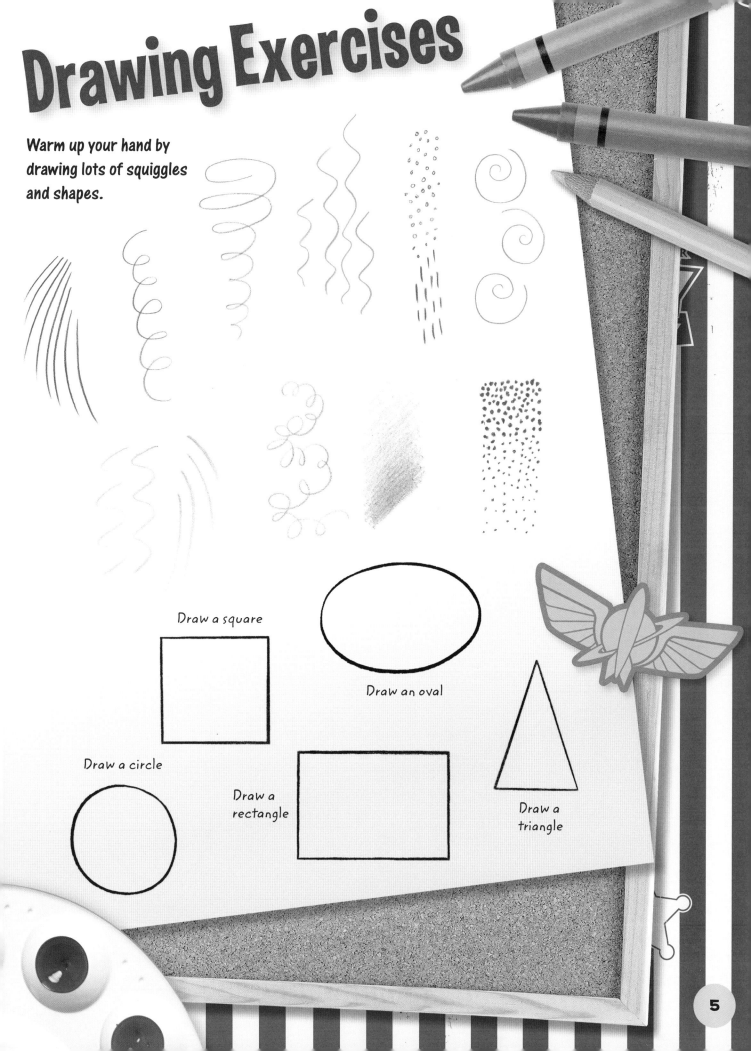

Draw a square

Draw an oval

Draw a circle

Draw a rectangle

Draw a triangle

WOODY

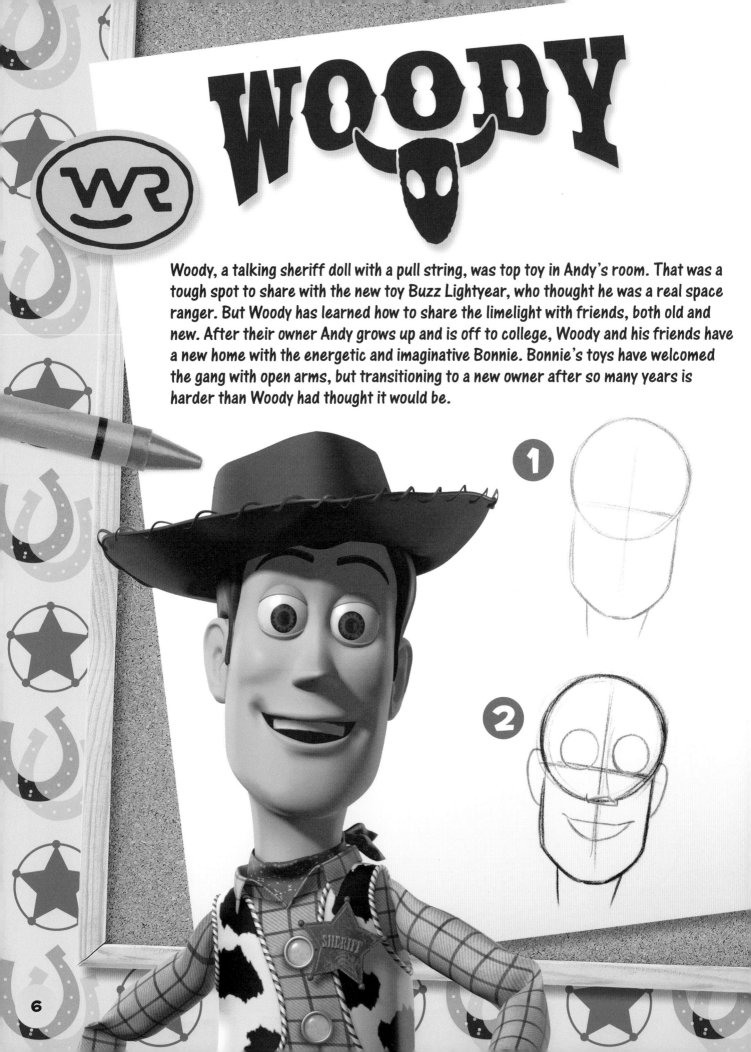

Woody, a talking sheriff doll with a pull string, was top toy in Andy's room. That was a tough spot to share with the new toy Buzz Lightyear, who thought he was a real space ranger. But Woody has learned how to share the limelight with friends, both old and new. After their owner Andy grows up and is off to college, Woody and his friends have a new home with the energetic and imaginative Bonnie. Bonnie's toys have welcomed the gang with open arms, but transitioning to a new owner after so many years is harder than Woody had thought it would be.

1

2

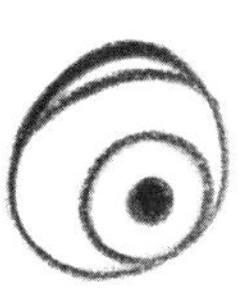

round eyes,
large iris

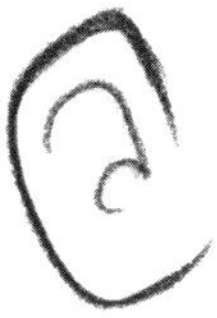

ears are flat
on top

3

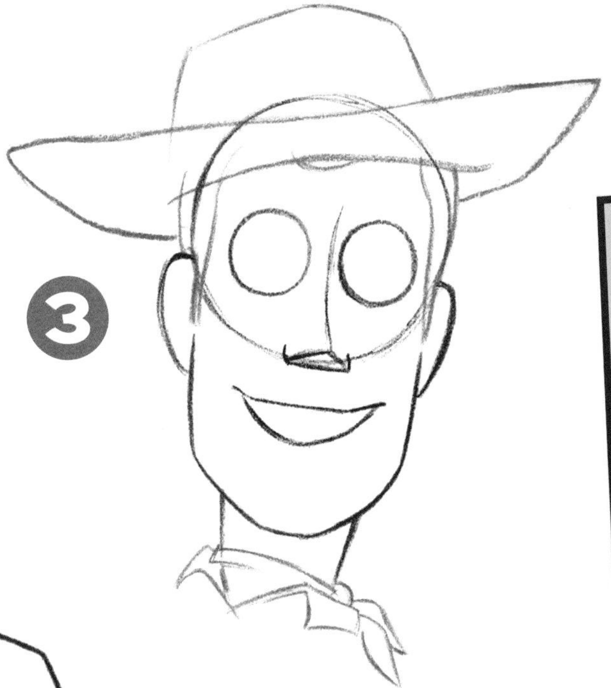

4

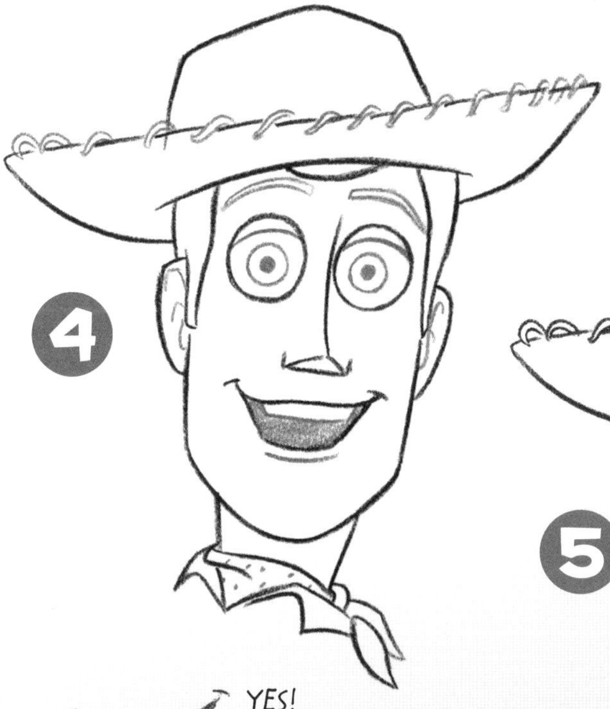

5

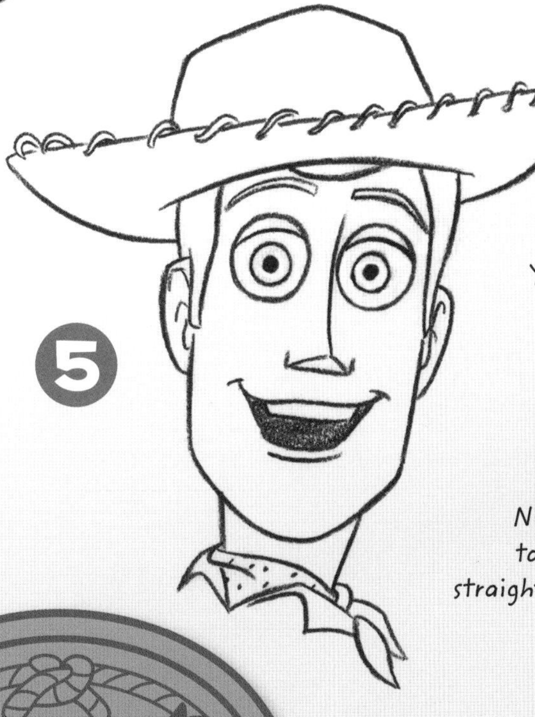

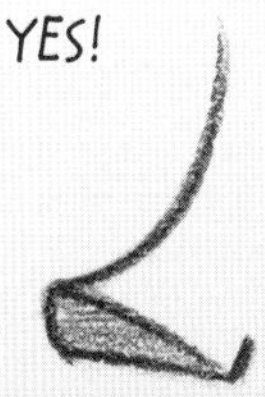

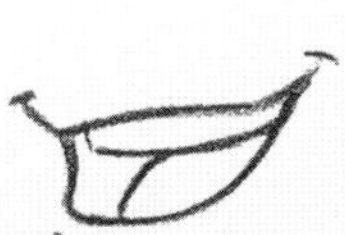

YES!
teeth are one long
rectangle

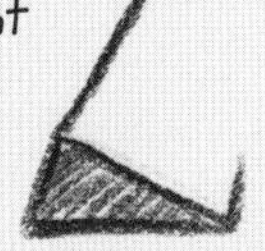

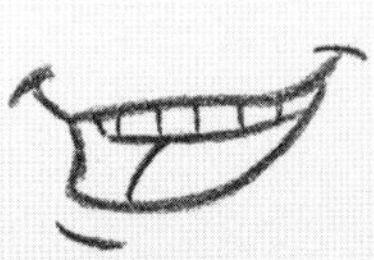

NO!

YES!

NO!
too
straight

BUZZ LIGHTYEAR

When Buzz Lightyear, Space Ranger, first joined the toys in Andy's room, he didn't understand that he was a toy. But Buzz learned his lesson well and sometimes has to remind Woody of what it means to be a toy! Transitioning from living with Andy to their new owner, Bonnie, was a big change, but Buzz has taken the move in stride. Though no longer the toy of the moment, Buzz is as bold and trustworthy as ever, always ready for a new adventure.

Buzz's chin takes up about 1/3 of his head

1

2

the chin cleft is 1/2 the distance between lower lip and chin

eyes can change shape in exaggerated expressions

3

chin cleft looks like the number 9

4

iris is about ⅓ the size of the eye

YES!   NO!

brow should barely touch eye in normal pose; keep brows thick

5

THE PROSPECTOR

The Prospector may seem like a nice, grandfatherly type of fellow at first, but when his true feelings are revealed, it becomes clear that he's just plain selfish and mean. Having never belonged to a child, the Prospector simply doesn't know how to play—or be loved.

mustache changes with mood

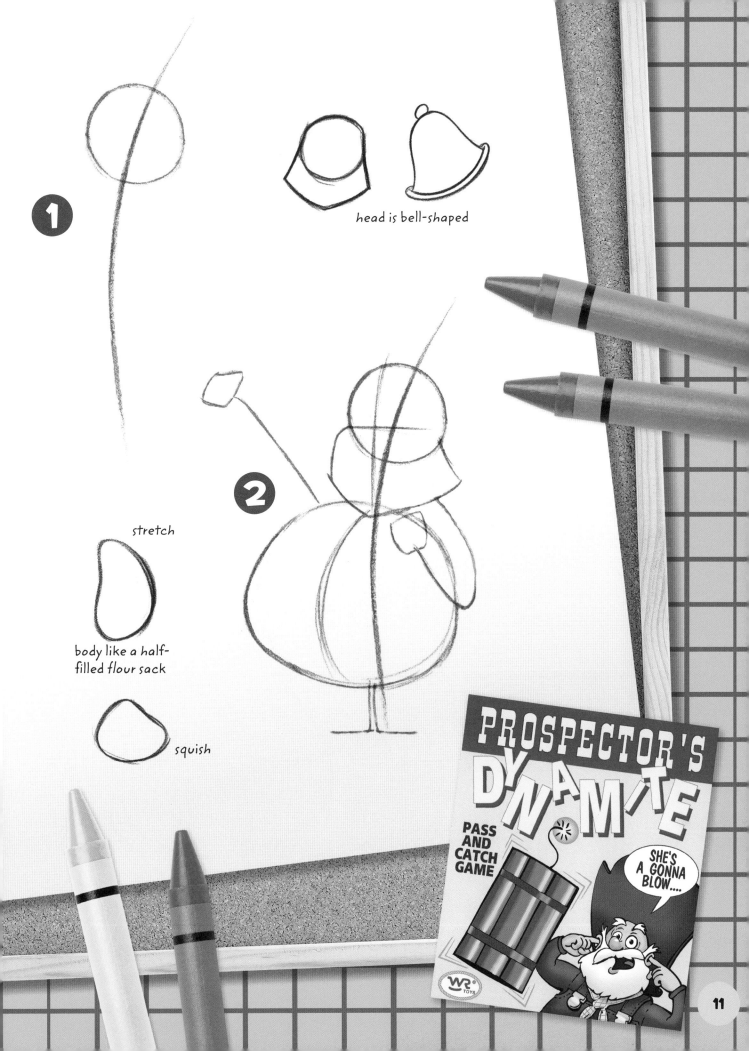

1

head is bell-shaped

2

stretch

body like a half-
filled flour sack

squish

PROSPECTOR'S
DYNAMITE

PASS
AND
CATCH
GAME

SHE'S
A GONNA
BLOW....

WR
TOYS

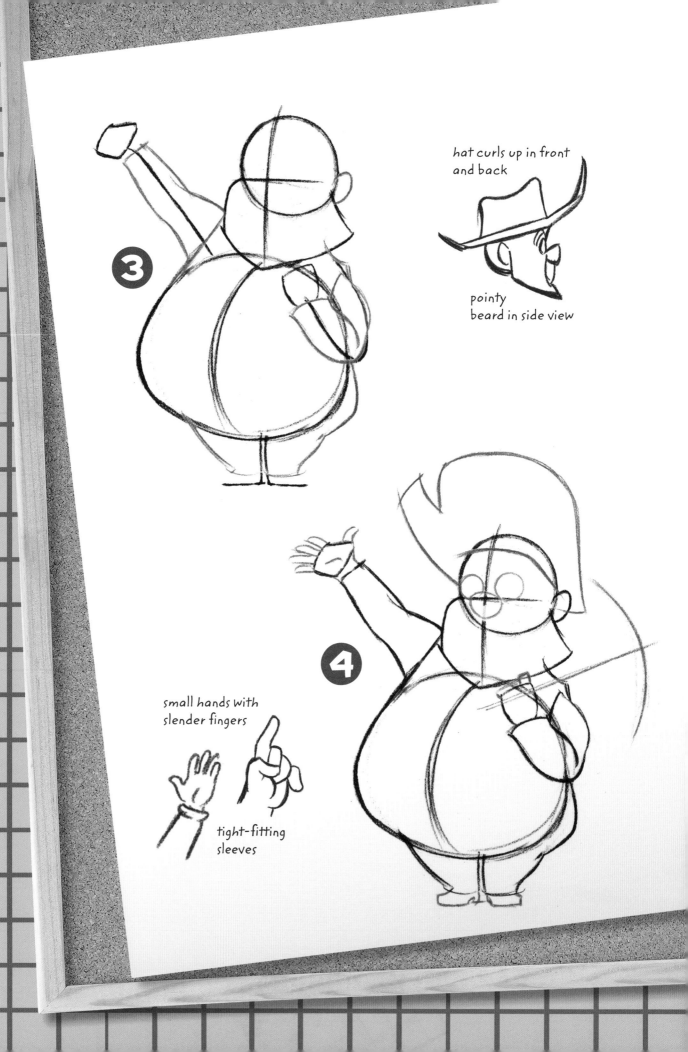

hat curls up in front
and back

pointy
beard in side view

small hands with
slender fingers

tight-fitting
sleeves

5

relaxed
gesture

excited
gesture

PROSPECTOR'S
DYNAMITE

PASS
AND
CATCH
GAME

SHE'S
A GONNA
BLOW....

the Prospector is
never without his
pickaxe

boot flares
at top

6

7

LOTSO

Lots-o'-Huggin' Bear—a.k.a Lotso—seems like nothing more than the nicest teddy bear at Sunnyside Daycare. But Lotso's true colors are exposed when he traps Andy's toys in the Caterpillar Room with all of the rambunctious toddlers—and later when he leaves the toys to be incinerated at the garbage dump.

1

ears are 2 half circles

2

eyebrows are
wide and bushy

YES!

NO!

I'M A
HUGGER

I'M A HUGGER

3

his cane is a wooden mallet

4

5

eyes are round
and set close
together

nose is an
upside-down
rounded
triangle

6

7

I'M A
HUGGER

8

teardrop-
shaped paws

BIG BABY

Big Baby (along with Lotso and Chuckles) was accidentally left at a rest stop by his first owner, Daisy. Although Big Baby initially does Lotso's dirty work at Sunnyside Daycare, once he realizes how much he misses his mama, he helps the toys escape from Lotso's grasp.

1

full lips YES!

NO!

Big Baby has
a curl on his
forehead

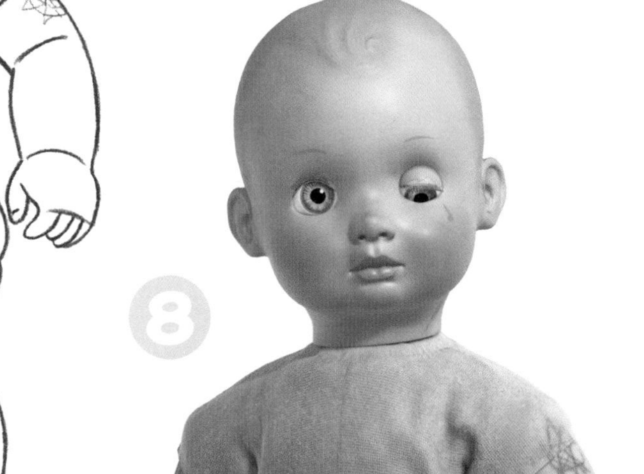

eyes are oval-shaped; his left
eye is broken and droops

CHUNK

Another of Lotso's cronies at Sunnyside Daycare, Chunk is a two-faced plastic rock monster who goes from friendly to foul with the punch of a button.

1

2

3

4

5

Chunk has two faces

6

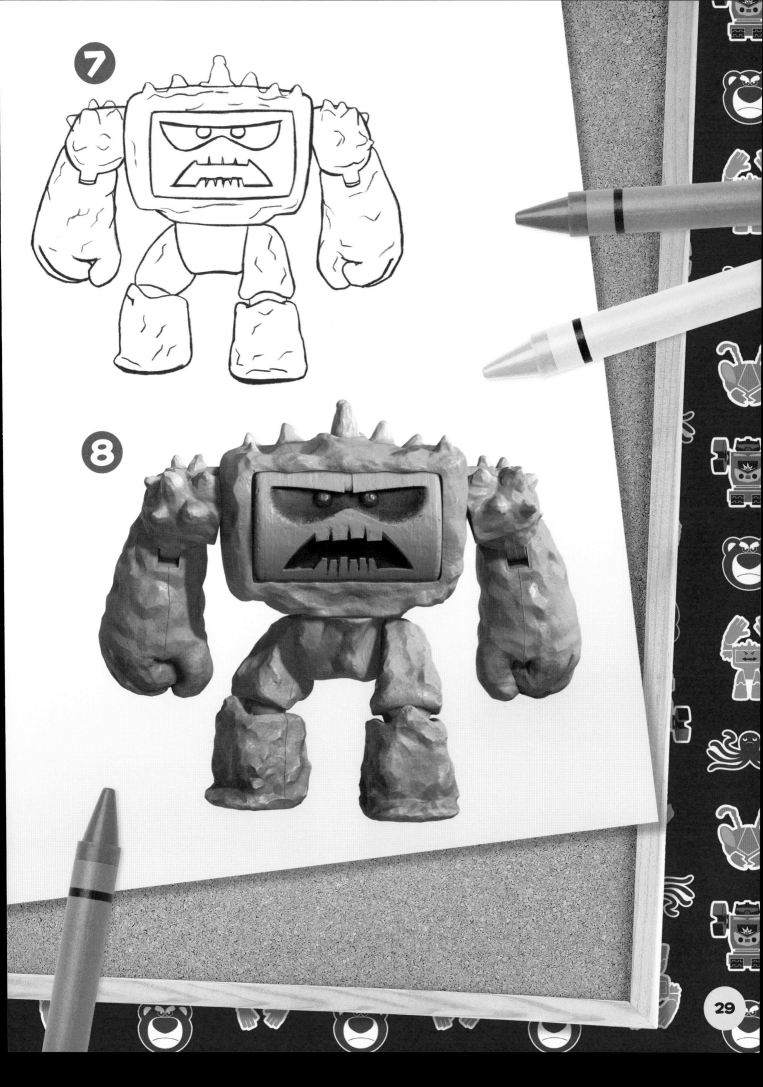

Mr. Pricklepants

Mr. Pricklepants is no ordinary hedgehog. This lederhosen-wearing toy is both dramatic and intellectual. He is also very kind to all of the other toys in Bonnie's toy collection.

Mr. Pricklepants is about ¹/₂ Woody's size

①

body looks like a pear

5

hat looks like an
upside-down cup
on a saucer

claws
are small
triangles

arms taper

6

7

8

suspenders
have a
buckle

Buttercup

Buttercup may look like a cute and cuddly unicorn, but he's really a gruff, no-nonsense member of Bonnie's toy collection.

1

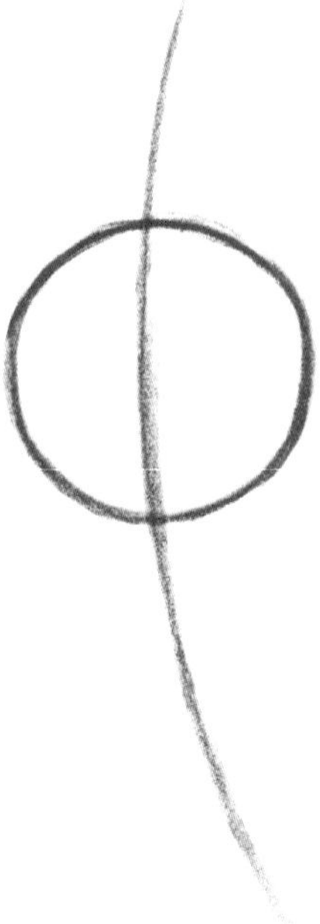

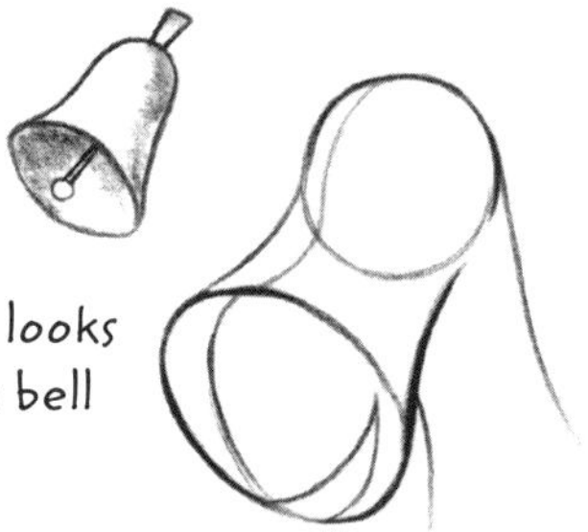

head looks like a bell

2

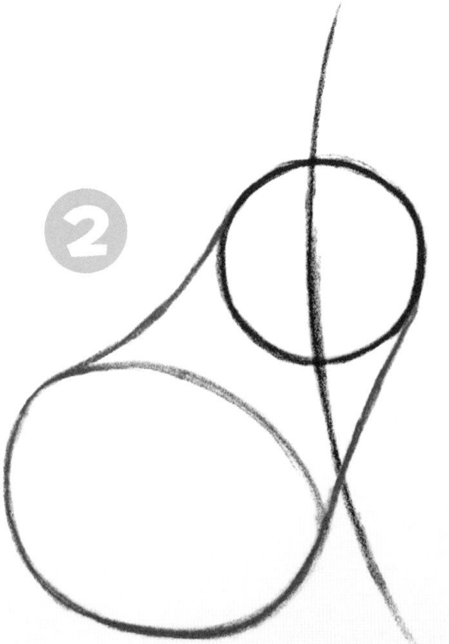

3

horn has 5 parts

4

tail is short
and bushy

5

eyes are ovals,
pupils and irises
are round, and
his eyebrows
follow the
shape of eye

6

body is drawn
from simple
shapes

nostrils
are heart-
shaped

BO PEEP

Bo Peep is a porcelain figurine who, along with her sheep, Billy, Goat, and Gruff, once decorated the base of a child's reading lamp. Don't let her delicate appearance fool you—Bo is as brave and tough as they come, with a dry sense of humor and lightning-quick reflexes. After Andy's sister, Molly, outgrew the lamp and gave it away, Bo and her sheep became "lost toys" by choice, traveling from town to town and helping others they meet along the way.

I'M IN CHARGE

39

Got it
HANDLED

5

I'M IN CHARGE

FORKY

Forky is a craft project created by Bonnie on the first day of kindergarten from a spork and art supplies. After being played with and coming to life, Forky has a lot of questions about his new existence as a toy.

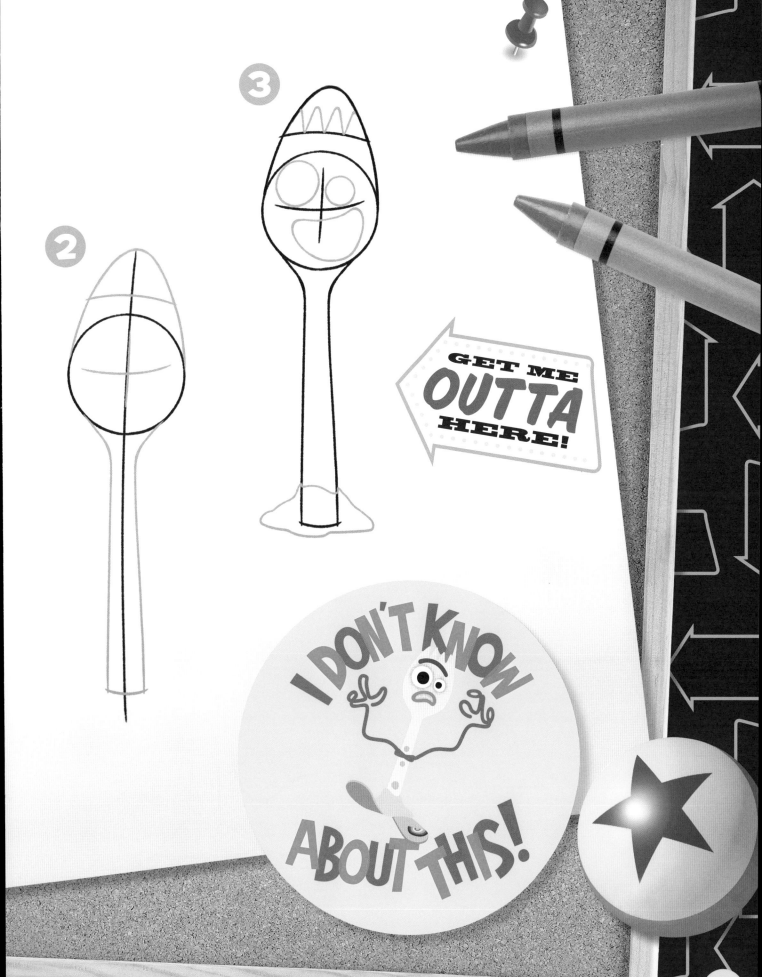

I'M HOMEMADE

DUKE CABOOM

Duke Caboom has all the swagger of Canada's greatest daredevil, but he's never quite recovered from being discarded by his kid after Duke's stunt cycle jumps turned out not to be as cool as advertised.

1

2

I'll jump
for you (ANYTIME!)

KABOOM!

③

④

I'll jump for you (ANYTIME!)

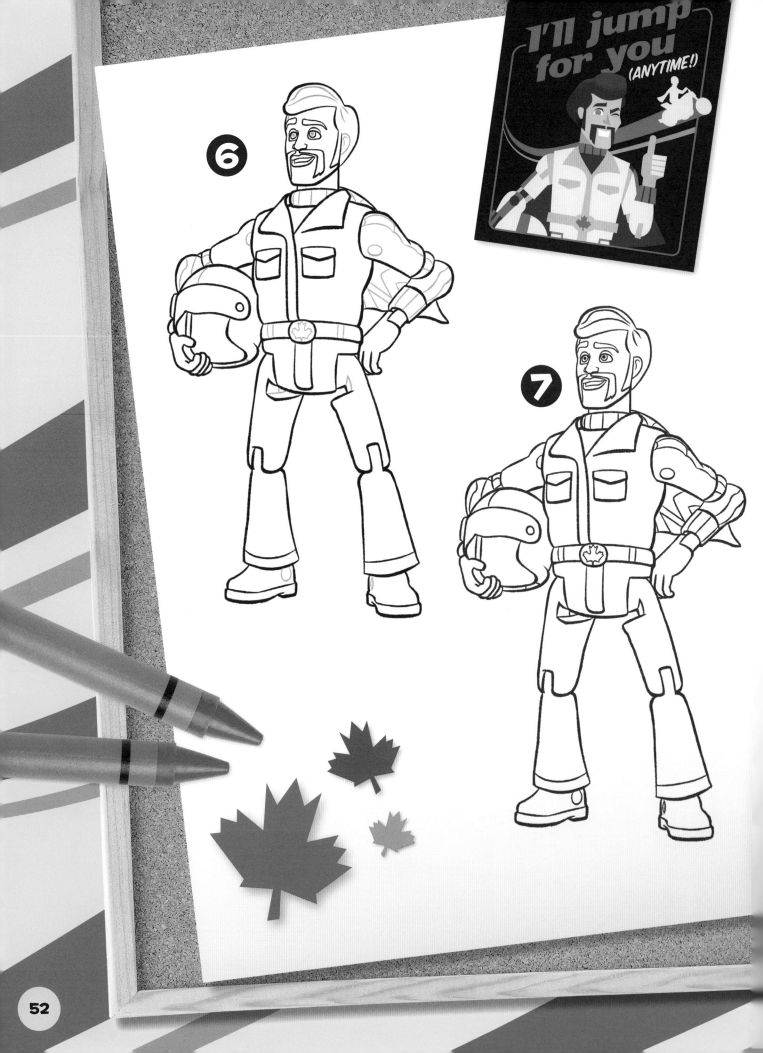

I'll jump for you (ANYTIME!)

6

7

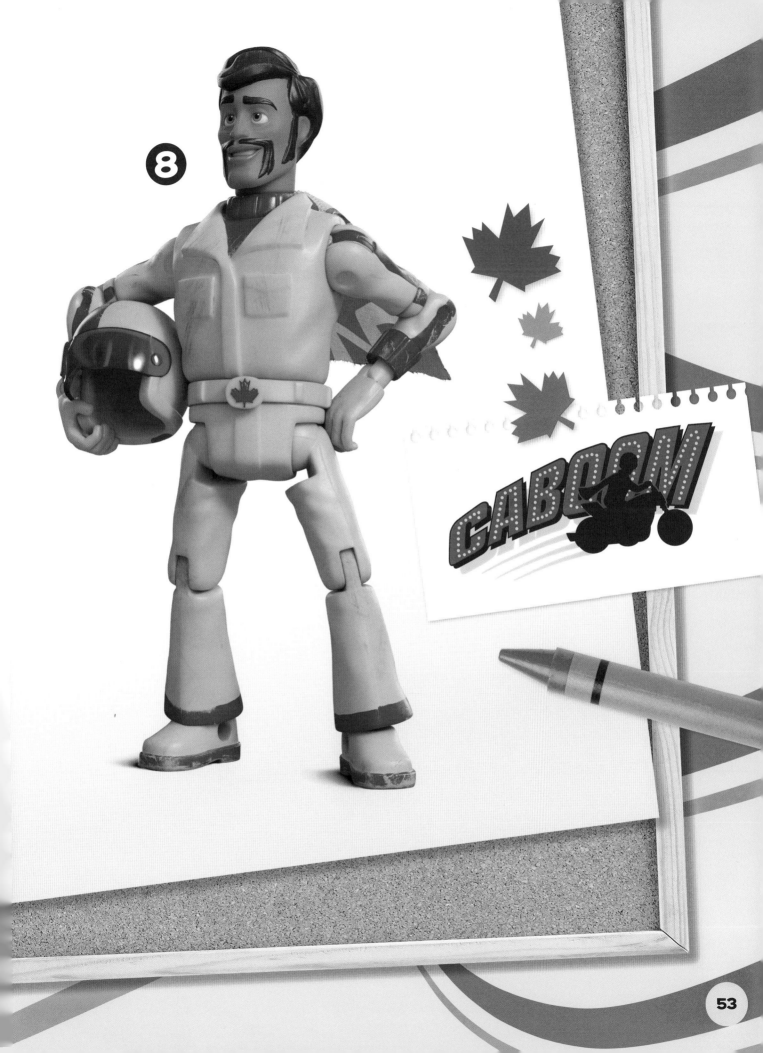

8

53

DUCKY & BUNNY

Ducky and Bunny are a pair of carnival-prize stuffed toys who are literally inseparable. They are attached to one another by their wing and paw. After hanging in a carnival game for years waiting to be won, their senses of humor are as sharp as ever.

You're
STUCK
with us!

STICK with US!

55

Gabby

Talking doll Gabby Gabby looks straight out of her original ads from the 1950s, but for some reason she's spent decades languishing in the glass display cabinet of an antiques store.

me

me

ALSO AVAILABLE FROM WALTER FOSTER JR.

**Learn to Draw
Disney•Pixar Toy Story:
Favorite Characters**
ISBN: 978-1-60058-833-4

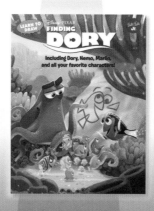

**Learn to Draw
Disney•Pixar
Finding Dory**
ISBN: 978-1-94287-518-5

**Learn to Draw
Disney•Pixar
Cars**
ISBN: 978-1-93958-144-0

Visit QuartoKnows.com for more Learn to Draw Disney books!